Poetic Philosophies-
A Collection of Ruminations and Contemplations in Poetry Style

Luke Mayo

Presentation by *BookLeaf Publishing*

Web: www.bookleafpub.com

E-mail: info@bookleafpub.com

ISBN: 9789358315189

First edition 2024

DEDICATION

This book is dedicated to the many, varied people who read it. May you look at the world with a critical mind and a discerning eye. May you enjoy what you see and, if you don't, may you do something positive about it.

ACKNOWLEDGEMENT

A great many people have influenced, nurtured, inspired and supported my life and creative efforts. I acknowledge some of them here and now.

The University of Suffolk, whose English department is and always will be a special part of my life's story. My work places and voluntary communities, especially Open Road Visions, who have supplied me with more material than my poetic mind knows what to do with.

And, of course, my family, the Mighty Clan of Mayo. They know my story, my struggles, my triumphs and my life better than anyone, as they were with me as I lived through it all. Their support made it possible.

Thank you all.

PREFACE

Most of us, at some stage in our lives, have a little think about the deeper things in life.

Why are we like this? Why do we do what we do? What's the meaning behind it all? Is there a reason? Am I thinking too hard? Am I not thinking hard enough?

For some of us, it's a passing thought. For others, it's a lifelong journey of discovery. This book of poems you're reading is the result of my own, personal ornate thinking. What might be deep and aesthetically pleasing for some, might also be redundant and obvious to other people.

In any case, here it is. Happy reading to you.

Pauses in the Hustle

Every day I'm hustling
 Except for the days I'm not

Working jobs
Paying bills
Seeing people
Doing chores
Repeat, repeat, repeat

Time taken
Energy expended

The moment I pause
Everything stops
Functions halt
Moments of nothing
Extending into more moments

Then I pick up and carry on

The flame burns bright and long
Then it snuffs out
The torch lights the way
Then it runs dry

Relatable
When you run dry
Stop
Then go again

First World Banality

Land far away
People at war
People in poverty
People sick and dying
People languishing in destruction

Then there's me
Food
Board
Clothes
Pocket money
Making the good days count
Sleeping the bad days off

Every uncomfy emotion
I cry it out
People understand
People relate
People sympathise

Then we move on
No harm done

All those people
Nowhere to turn

No friends to share
Hell is the only company

The story of my life
Sometimes naff but otherwise ok

Won't Stop Yapping

The creative folks
Always something to say
Always something to share
Endless responses to the human condition
Helping us to process it all

An occupational hazard
Being told to shut up
Pipe down
Stay quiet
Button it
Stop yapping

Those who don't understand
Those who disagree
Those who stir trouble
Those who make waves
Those who are jealous
Those who have nothing to contribute

They oppose the creatives
They know no way but to obstruct
They snuff out all light and warmth

They only stop us if we let them

We won't stop yapping
Our voices speak still
We will always create

The Turning of my Mind

Rising like a sun over the horizon
 Turning like a planet on its axis
 Forging ahead like a meteor through the cosmos

This is my mind

Happy feelings
Oppressive feelings
Stale feelings
No feelings

They come
They sit awhile
They bask in my presence
And I in theirs
Engaging in each other's' existence

Then they go
Replaced by something new
They stay not the same
Nor remain in place
Thank goodness for that

Be open to change
It may be an opinion

It may be a belief
It may be a worldview

Anything is possible
Our feelings do not govern us
We are their owners
We call the shots

The choice is ours always

Storms Through Winter

Christmas time brings so much
Like snowflakes on the breeze
Like unified voices carolling through the night
Like the love of friends through thick and thin
So too comes yuletide joy

Something else appears this time of year
The haunting presence of seasonal depression

Dark hours
Darker emotions
Long nights
Longer silences
Sunlight through the wintry mists
The warmth draws not near me

One thing we know
Winter ends
Spring begins
What once despaired in frozen wastelands
Finds its place in sunny meadows

As is for the seasons
So too for humanity
All you have to do is wait

Winter's emotional storms will pass
Spring's hopeful sun will rise

Make sure you're there to greet it
I'll be there too
Let our survival of winter unite us
Bond our friendship
Guide us on through spring to summer glory

Thankful for the Sunset

Like a beacon lighting the darkest sea
 The sunset spreads across the evening sky

More wondrous than fireworks
Twice the beauty
Much less the noise

Though the dark night lies ahead
The beautiful act of nature is now
May as well enjoy it while I can
Because I can
Because it's lovely

A sunset leads to nightfall
Nightfall goes forth to daybreak
The ongoing cycle of light's rests and rises
The sunset harkens nature's faithful presence

The sunset is impermanent
Impermanence diminishes not the beauty
Just take a look
Soak in the wonder
Let it inspire you
The sight won't last
Your happy memory will

Sunset
I thank you
Your light brightens the night

Shielded from Everything

Every day
Every place
People walk past people
They interact with a smile
Then they move on

How little they all know
They've all been brutalised
Traumatised
Scarred, battered and bruised

We wear our masks
Raise our barricades
Refuging behind our armour

We've been used
We've been betrayed
We've been beaten
We've been mocked
We've been abandoned

Not that anyone else would know

We hide behind smiles
Laughs

Bravado
The machismo typical of our age

And that's those of us who are decent

The bullies
The hooligans
The raging psychos
Believe it or not
They've been hurt worst of all
That's why they hide it so well

We wear different shields
We hide different injuries
We are united by one thing

Our need for a shield

Waters of My Life

15

Come walk with me by the river
It's a good life here

All the places I go
Jobs and friends
Events of my life
I walk along the river to reach them

I played here as a child
Imagination running wild
Worlds of possibility

Sometimes company would join me here
Friends of mine sharing the walk
Birds and animals coming to meet me
Sharing this place by the river

So many memories
Alighting my face with a smile
Those memories and that light
Finding their source at the river

This is my place
My life
My home

Those who share it with me
I love your company

The Unseen Folks

A world of commerce
A world of entertainment
A world of humanity

This is our world

We live our lives
We do our thing
Working our jobs
Having a laugh
Day after day
Repeating the process

As the days go by
It becomes increasingly clear
All is not as it seems

Those at the top
Those hidden away
Those pulling the strings
Those calling the shots
Those leading the way

How little we know
How little we see

They are camouflaged
They avoid being seen

Thus they carry on
Putting things in place
Setting things in motion
Charting the course of humanity
All from behind the scenes

They have money
They have power
They have influence
Anonymity is how they maintain it

We know they're here
Silent acknowledgement
Our world continues like this

Mentally Adrift

Sometimes
When I live my life
It's just my body living it
Doing my job
Having conversations

Where's my mind?
Where indeed

Casting back
So many memories
Some of them pleasant
Some of them horrific

My mind floats over them all
Like a cloud over a meadow
While my body does what it does
My mind is perpetually elsewhere

Hours and days of my life
Ruminating on what's happened
Contemplating what may happen
Mysteries of the universe
Undiscovered wonders
My mind explores them

Then my mind returns to my body
Realises what it's missed
Mind and body make their journey together
Ready to make more memories

The next time my mind goes adrift
I wonder where it will go?

Shelter from the World

For the length of human history
One thing remains the same
We are a brutal race

Wars
Hate crimes
Terrorism
Bullying
Trolling

It's a good thing we've found shelters

Safety from the hatred
Refuge from the violence
Respite from each other

Finding a way to end the horror
Working towards peace
Striving for resolution
That's what shelter is there for

Is it the world we're sheltering from?
Or is it human beings?

Either way

Shelters are blessings
The progression of humanity
The achievement of goodness
Together as one here

Instead of attacking each other
What if we shelter each other?

Can you imagine?

Bodily Battleground

Every human
Every day
We go to war

Fighting for rights
Squabbling over resources
Scrabbling for a place
Screaming for answers

The most basic and personal fight of all
Fighting for our health

Our bodies
Every moment that passes
Fending off an onslaught
Germs
Microbes
Viruses
Infections

All these forms of life
Encroaching on our own lives
Potentially endangering them
And so the fight back ensues

Weapons at our disposal
Medicines
Pills
Vaccines

The trouble is
They might
Just might
Cause more problems than they cure

Do we take the risk?
Do we encourage others to take the risk?
What's right?
What's wrong?
Will we ever know?

We can only keep fighting

Self-care
Care for others
However is best to do this
Make sure you do it

Where Will We Be?

Look around you
Friends
Co-workers
Homesteads
Happy memories

Look ahead
The fog of uncertainty

One step at a time
Steps become miles
Moments become years
Living through time

Now look around
All those people
All those places
All those memories

They've changed
What once was is gone
What is now is different

The places we are
The places we'll be

Constantly evolving

What we now know
What we now assume
Taking for granted
Keep an eye on it
It may not stay

Ever-changing reality
Where will it lead us?

Between Dreams and Actions

Family members
Career counsellors
Close friends
Saying the same thing
"Follow your dreams"

Sounds good
Sounds positive
Sounds affirmational

Just one question
How does that work?

What if my dream is bogus?
What if my dream is a mistake?
What if my dream is unrealistic?
What if I don't even have a dream?

Life hurls obstacles at me
Life leads a different way
Life keeps me in the dark

Those dreams
Not yet reality
They can become real

I need to learn how

Learn what action to take
Learn what support is available
Lean what the consequences will be

Transitioning between dreams and reality
A worthy path to take

In Love With Love

"My life and death will be for you"
"Every fibre of my existence is yours"
"I begin and end with your embrace"

What is this love of yours?
It is love itself
Or maybe the idea of love

Those who need a relationship
Those who depend on the company of another
Those who pour their devotion into someone's
soul

Even if it's repaid with violence
Even if it's repaid with manipulation
Even if it's not repaid at all

This they prefer to being alone

What do you fear more?
Having no other people?
Having people who do every bad thing to you?

What if you treated yourself right?

What if you found people who also treated you
right?
What if you removed the people who did
wrong?

Love is love
Love does not treat you badly
Love is love
Love is not selfish
Love is love
Love does not tolerate appalling behaviour

Love is great
That's why you shouldn't force it from others
That's why you should have some for yourself

See You, See Me

A life based on looking
This is the life we all have

How do you see yourself?
How do you see others?
How do others see you?
How do others see themselves?

Questions with so many answers
As many answers as people on the planet

Where some see strength
Others see stubbornness
Where some see courage
Others see idiocy
Where some see rights
Others see comforts

Some find you funny
Some find you wise
Some find you banal
Some find you irritating
Some don't find you at all

All equally valid and meaningless

We are united in who we are
We are unique in our perceptions

What a complex people we are

Our First Kiss

It was the toughest night of my life
It was also the most heavenly

Leaving the house at 10PM
Normally I'd be tucked away in bed
On to the bars and nightclubs
The last places on earth you'd find me
Bright lights and loud noises
Explosions for the senses

A long and ongoing ordeal
Made worthwhile by one thing
You and your kiss

It was soft
It was heartfelt
It was smooth
It was endless

We fell into each other's embrace
We held on to each other with gentle hands
We shared warmth
We shared love
We shared passion

On through the night
Cheesy chips at 3AM
Late supper or early breakfast
Doesn't matter either way

That kiss is all that matters

The victory of the night's fight
The reward for being out of the comfort zone
That's what our kiss means to me

Escaping Judgement

I live my life
I try different things
I inhabit different personas

Some things go great
Some things are loved
Some things fail badly
Some things are intensely hated

When those things are done
They are set in stone by their witnesses

Those who saw me succeed
I'm their hero
I'm their best friend
Those who saw me flounder
I am their loser
I am their pathetic waste of space

I keep trying different things
I am still all those things to those people
I always will be
They assign me their place for me
It will never change
It is what it is

Every mistake I ever made
Every slip-up
Every misjudgement
Every bad moment
Those people are my jailers
Those memories are my jail

How little they know
I escape with my actions
Their perception is forever trapped in the past
My life is not
It's not me they imprison
It's their own mind

I go on
I keep trying
They won't stop me
Their judgement sinks not its claws into my
soul

They don't move on with me
That's why they're not here any more

Life changes always
Even if we don't let ourselves change with it